# Old-Time

s

## for

## Clawhammer Banjo

by Dan Levenson

## Contents - Audio 1 - Banjo Versions; Audio 2 - Fiddle Versions

1. And the Cat Came Back
2. Angelina Baker
3. Arkansas Traveler
4. Bitter Creek
5. Black Hills Waltz
6. Bob Tailed Mule
7. Bonapart's Retreat
8. Booth Shot Lincoln
9. Briar Picker Brown
10. Cluck Old Hen
11. Cold Frosty Morning - modal
12. Cold Frosty Morning - major
13. The Cuckoo
14. Cumberland Gap
15. Doctor Doctor
16. Duck River
17. Ducks on the Milpond
18. Ebenezer
19. (Mr.) Fishar's Hornpipe - 3 part version
20. Folding Down the Sheets
21. Forked Deer
22. Fortune
23. Great Big 'Taters in a Sandy Land
24. Grey Eagle
25. Johnson Boys
26. Katy Hill
27. Little Dutch Girl
28. The Merry Blacksmith
29. Mississippi Sawyer
30. (Wooliver's) Money Musk
31. Needlecase
32. Old Belle Cow
33. Opera Reel
34. Over the Waterfall
35. Policeman
36. Polly Put the Kettle On
37. Push the Pig's Foot a Little Further Into the Fire
38. The Rattlesnake
39. Rock the Cradle Joe
40. Sal's Got Mud Between Her Toes
41. Salt Creek (aka Salt River)
42. Salty River Reel
43. Shady Grove - modal version
44. (Doc Robert's) Shortnin' Bread
45. Snowbird
46. Soldier's Joy
47. Spotted Pony
48. Step Around Johnny
49. Sugar Hill
50. Three Thin Dimes
51. Three Way Hornpipe
52. Waiting for the Federals (aka Seneca Square Dance)
53. Walk Along John to Kansas
54. Walking in the Parlor
55. Westfork Gals
56. Whitesburg
57. (There is a) Wild Hog in the Woods
58. Wild Horses at Stony Point
59. Wooden Nickel
60. The Year of Jubilo (aka Lincoln's Gunboats)
61. Yellow Barber
62. Y. Z. Hamilton's Special Breakdown

Online Audio    www.melbay.com/30224BCDEB

1 2

**Visit us on the Web at www.melbay.com — E-mail us at e-mail@melbay.com**

# Dedication

To my wife, Jennifer Levenson, who has been a true inspiration and rock of support as I make the journey called life through a musical path.

To my students who have supported me and my materials for so many years.

To my publisher, Mel Bay, the family and workers there who make this available to you and give my musical writings voice to the world.

# Table of Contents

Dedication.................................................2

Introduction...............................................4

About the CDs...........................................4

About the Tunes.........................................5

About Written Music..................................5

Reading the Tablature................................6

A Final Note of Encouragement.................7

And the Cat Came Back...............................8

Angelina Baker..........................................10

Arkansas Traveler.....................................12

Bitter Creek...............................................14

Black Hills Waltz.......................................18

Bob Tailed Mule........................................20

Bonapart's Retreat - Wm. H. Stepp version.......22

Booth Shot Lincoln...................................24

Briar Picker Brown....................................26

Cluck Old Hen...........................................28

Cold Frosty Morning - modal - Henry Reed; Mel Durham version.........................30

Cold Frosty Morning - major - Melvin Wine version.......................................32

The Cuckoo...............................................34

Cumberland Gap.......................................36

Doctor Doctor...........................................38

Duck River................................................40

Ducks on the Millpond.............................42

Ebenezer..................................................44

(Mr.) Fishar's Hornpipe - 3 part version...........46

Folding Down the Sheets..........................48

Forked Deer..............................................50

Fortune.....................................................52

Great Big Taters in A Sandy Land............54

Grey Eagle.................................................56

Johnson Boys............................................58

Katy Hill...................................................60

Little Dutch Girl.......................................62

The Merry Blacksmith..............................64

Mississippi Sawyer...................................66

(Wooliver's) Money Musk.........................68

Needlecase................................................70

Old Belle Cow...........................................72

Opera Reel................................................74

Over the Waterfall....................................76

Policeman.................................................78

Polly Put the Kettle On............................80

Push the Pig's Foot a Little Further Into the Fire................................................82

The Rattlesnake........................................84

Rock the Cradle Joe..................................86

Sal's Got Mud Between Her Toes..............88

Salt Creek - aka Salt River.......................90

Salty River Reel........................................92

Shady Grove - modal version...................94

(Doc Robert's) Shortnin' Bread................96

Snowbird.................................................100

Soldier's Joy............................................102

Spotted Pony...........................................104

Step Around Johnny................................106

Sugar Hill................................................108

Three Thin Dimes...................................110

Three Way Hornpipe...............................112

Waiting For the Federals - aka Seneca Square Dance...........................114

Walk Along John to Kansas.....................116

Walking in the Parlor..............................118

West Fork Gals.........................................120

Whitesburg..............................................122

(There is a) Wild Hog in the Woods.......124

Wild Horses at Stony Point.....................126

Wooden Nickel.........................................128

The Year of Jubilo - aka Lincoln's Gunboats...130

Yellow Barber..........................................132

Y. Z. Hamilton's Special Breakdown........134

Other products by Dan Levenson.............138

About Dan................................................140

# Introduction

Welcome to *Old Time Favorites for Clawhammer Banjo*. First, let me be clear that this book is intended to be a tune repertoire book and not a primary instruction book. For that I would direct you to my book *Clawhammer Banjo From Scratch* (Mel Bay 20190 BCD) and the corresponding DVDs (MB 5003), which are also available from Mel Bay Publications. It has been a book that my students have said is a must for anyone learning to play the *clawhammer* banjo style as well as anyone with a desire to improve their playing skills, no matter what level you are.

This book, *Old Time Favorites for Clawhammer Banjo*, presents over 60 tunes for you to play. Most of these are old time favorites that are well known and often show up at many of the jam sessions you are likely to become part of. Some are cliché, others unusual, some easy, some difficult. Some have been in previous publications but are enhanced here to allow more variety and musical development than before.

It has been some 15 years since I first wrote *Buzzard Banjo – Clawhammer Style* (Mel Bay 99126) containing 25 tablature transcriptions which I originally self published in a copy shop comb binding and line art card stock paper cover. It was my first book ever and even though I had to learn to write tablature in order to produce it, folks have told me that they were (are) amazed at how playable and like real music those tabs were.

That book was soon picked up by Mel Bay Publications and released with the original tabs plus the added CD of 50 tracks – with a slow and up to speed version of each tune played by me for you to listen to as a reference and a nice glossy cover featuring a photo of me that was taken by my younger son, Joshua. That was in the year 2000. It has been a long road since then.

To this day, I still thank Richard *Bubba Hutch* Hutchison for taking the time to teach me to write tab and keep watch on me while I did the first ones at his home then in Houston, Texas. Bubba had been transcribing my playing from cassette recordings and sending them to *Banjo Newsletter* magazine for publication. It was his lead and encouragement that made that first book happen. He passed away a few years ago and I can tell you he is missed. Somehow, his spirit has kept me writing this music for you through Mel Bay Publications and as a writer and now editor for *Banjo Newsletter* and its quarterly *Old Time Way* insert dedicated to old time banjo playing including the clawhammer style.

As I look over the now 10 books before this one (which include fiddle and mandolin publications as well as clawhammer banjo) I have become fascinated by the development of both the style of transcriptions and my playing which I can see as I have written the tabs and music for this book. From a single line of tablature to the current format where I provide standard notation as well as basic and advanced lines of tablature offering you more choices and insight of what to play, I still wish I could provide more *music* for you as opposed to just more notes. BUT, that is what YOUR development is supposed to be all about.

## About the CDs

There are 2 CDs accompanying this volume. I decided that what would serve you best is a single interpretive composite version of each tune played on *banjo* and another on *fiddle* all at a moderate speed so you can *hear* the tunes as well as read them. These are NOT an exact playing of what has been written but a more *real life* representation of the tunes and essentially 4th and 5th versions of each tune for you to work on by ear. Playing by ear is an important skill in traditional music.

The recorded *banjo version* will sound more full than the single note version as the tunes are written.

That is to say, there is more fill or what some call the *crash and noise* that is often heard in one's playing but not written out. That is because while the written music is literal, played and heard music is less intentional. Also, having the recorded *fiddle version* will give you a more literal base to work from and be like what you hear in local jam sessions.

## About the Tunes

Each tune presented here has the following characteristics:

*A chord line* - The chord names are printed above the standard notation line at each chord change or at the beginning of each part. Chords are not so intuitive or fixed as most folks would believe and are therefore often in dispute. I use the *don't encourage bad music* rule. Just because the old timers might not have known a better chord than they used doesn't mean theirs was the best choice or that it sounded good. Use your judgment here as in all music. Use what you like, like what you use. I like mine but fully acknowledge there are other, perhaps better options.

*Standard notation* - Folks wanted a melody line that would be playable by those who don't play or need banjo tab. It is indicative of the tab version but is only a point of reference and beginning, not a master that is slavishly reproduced by the tab. It's a good starting point and is used as the reference for this book and for its fiddle and mandolin companion titled, oddly enough, *Old Time Favorites for Fiddle and Mandolin* (MB 30225).

*Basic tablature line* - This line should be playable by all but the most beginning players. While it is intended to be basic it is not a *baby* version of the tune. These versions of the tunes usually follow at least the basic melody. I strive to minimize drop thumb moves and unusual playing techniques in this tab line. Even so, there will be times when the *basic* version just isn't so easy and perhaps even more difficult for some of you than the *advanced* version below it.

*Advanced tablature line* - This line should provide some challenges to most everyone. It will require more time and finesse as it is usually more *ornamental* (*more* than just *melodic*) and may include some less than intuitive ways of playing some passages. It even surprised me to see some of my fingering written out in tab. It is pretty much the most intricate version of the tune. This version contains more hammers-ons, pull-offs, double and drop thumbs. This line may or may *NOT* agree with the basic and standard notation lines. That is partly because of other techniques used including counter melody, blue notes and syncopation. You can also expect to find hammer-ons and pull-offs to un-played strings and what is commonly referred to as the *Galax lick*, which is indicated by one full beat drawn out finger stroke followed by a full beat long thumbed note.

## About Written Music

Please remember that written music has many limits when it comes to accurately representing true *music*. There are many subtleties and inflections that cannot really be represented by the limited palette that written music provides. Also, in one written pass through any tune, there are countless variations of notes and techniques that likely would not ALL be played in one playing of the tune. This is done so you have as many options as possible to choose from when you play the tune. Learn the written music, but listen to the CD versions, too. Find older (I often look for the oldest) sources whenever you can. If you listen long enough, you will find that you can sing the tune before you ever try to play it. Which brings me to:

*Creativity* - Beyond The *Right* (Write) way - My version will *not* be the only version you come upon as you journey through the old time music world. These versions of the tunes come from how I hear and play music that has been handed down for generations and CHANGED for many reasons by each player that has handled and played each tune. Mine are not supposed to be the only one you always want to play or hear. You get to put your own variations in as well. A and B parts may be one way here, and reversed in your jam session. Some folks may play only one A and others 2. Tune titles may vary. You may want to make a crooked tune come out even for a dance.

These transcriptions are intended to be a *starting* point, not an ending. In reality, there is no one right way to play any of these tunes. Everything is open to your interpretation. If there is a right way it is the way you like it. *HOWEVER*, if you are going to play with others - a goal of most but not all folks - then the right way will be the one you agree on in your group no matter how large or small. With more licks in your bag of tricks, you will be most able to adapt to the music of the day and time.

# Reading the Tab

This book is written in standard notation and a type of music notation known as tablature. Reading tablature is in many ways easier than reading music. In tablature the lines of the staff indicate the strings of the banjo and the notes are numbers that tell you the fret numbers on each string.

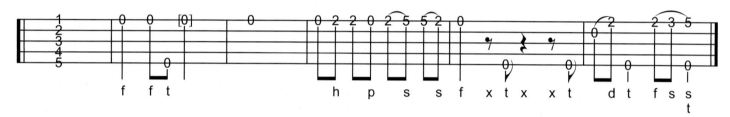

In tablature, the top line of the staff represents the first string of your banjo and the bottom line the 5th (short) string. The second measure shows some of the notes used. A quarter note counts as 1 beat (say, "one"). Eighth notes count as 1/2 beat each so, 2 eighth notes = one quarter note (say, "one and") and a half note counts for 2 beats or 2 times a quarter note (say, "one and two and"). The next measure shows a whole note, which counts as 4 beats (say, "one and two and three and four and"). A dot ( ˙ ) next to the note adds half the value of the note to the time of that note (i.e. a quarter note is one beat, a quarter note followed by the dot is *one and a half* beats).

The letters under the note symbols will indicate whether you use the finger - "f" or the thumb - "t" of your right hand to play the note. An "x" indicates silence and means that you don't play this note. Your hand keeps moving up and down even though you are not sounding a note.

The h, p and s give playing directions for your left hand. The "h" is the symbol for a hammer-on, the "p" is the symbol for a pull-off and the "s" indicates a slide. I also use a "slur" (the curve above the notes) for the slide. Notes with no marking under them should fit the rule that if the note is on the first half of the beat, it is played with your finger. If on the second half of the beat, it is played with your thumb or is a hammer on, slide, or pull off.

*The Galax Lick* – This name is the common name given to a move where you actually roll two beats with the finger and thumb where each gets a full beat instead of the usual half beat for each. Your finger plays the first notes of the series with the down stroke of your hand in a delayed motion taking a full beat. It can be a single note, a hammer on or slide on that string or it might require you to drag ("d") the finger stroke across the multiple strings – then with a continued motion as your hand circles back up the thumb plays the fifth string. That puts the fifth string sounding at the beginning of the second beat instead of the end of the first one. You are actually taking 2 beats to complete the down-up hand motion of clawhammer playing instead of the usual one beat. Two types of this lick are shown in the last measure of the example above.

# A Final Note of Encouragement

There are no mistakes, only notes you didn't intend to play. If you find you played a note or phrase differently from the written music and you like it, cool. If you play a note you don't like, well, don't play that one next time.

Music is to be enjoyed by all and expressive of your soul. Don't be afraid to play it *your* way but don't be reluctant to experiment or try someone else's version either.

Play alone or play together.

Whatever you choose and your community or musical partner agree on is fine. Just...

## Play Nice!

Play Nice!

# And the Cat Came Back

# Angelina Baker
## aka Angeline the Baker

Double D tuning
aDADE (double C capo 2)

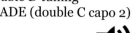

Track 2

10

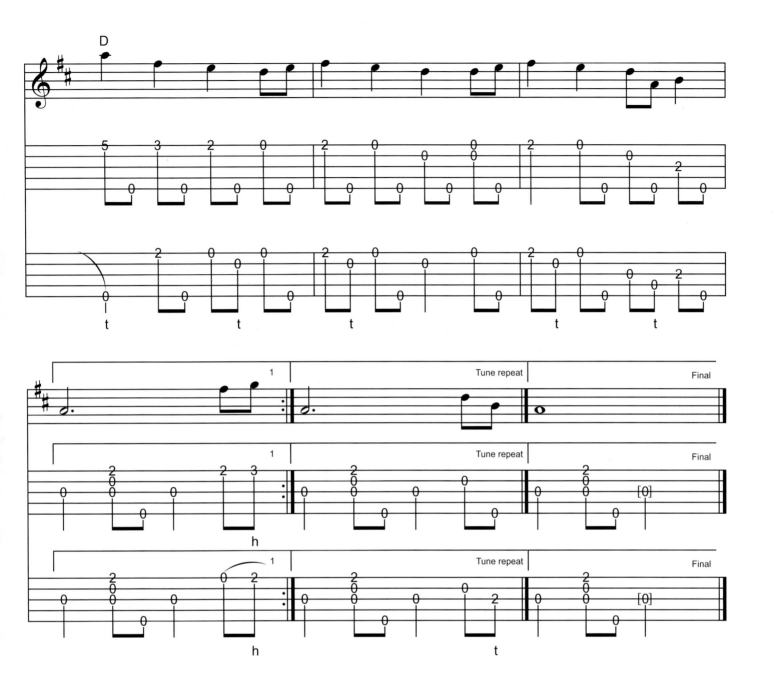

# Arkansas Traveler

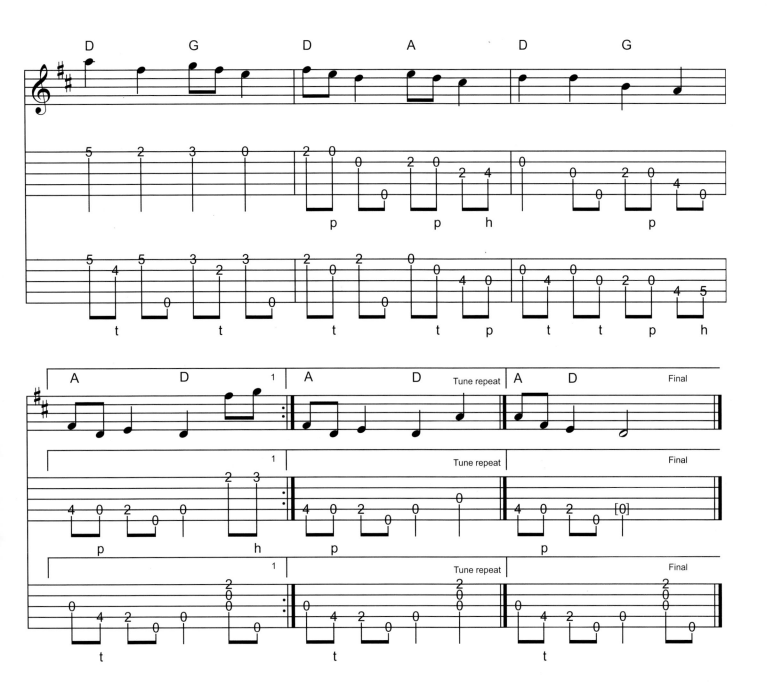

# Bitter Creek

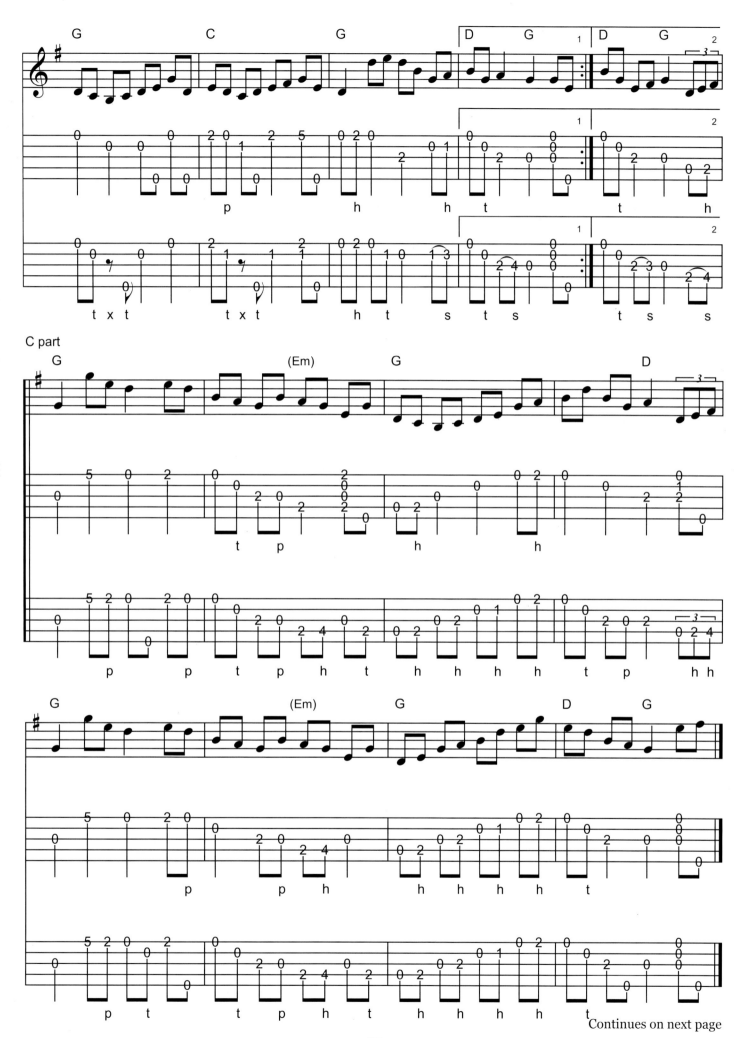

C part

Continues on next page

15

Sorry, I just couldn't keep this on a two-page spread. There are so many variations of the number of times folks play a part that this was the only way to give you enough to explore all of the possibilities. Many consider fiddler *Benny Thomasson's* version to be *the* way to play this tune and that is the version I have based the standard notation line on.

I've written the parts out pretty much as my band, *The Boiled Buzzards,* played it on our recording, *Early Bird Special* (Buzzard CD 1004) with two A parts, two B parts and one each C and D.

*Benny* usually played each part twice but not always. Benny's former neighbor and my fiddle buddy here in AZ - Don *Dexter* Poindexter really mixes it up and plays the parts AA-B-C-DD-B - well, that's how he did it in one recording anyway. In actuality, he varies it a bit each time he plays it.

*Art Stamper* usually played each part twice as well. *Charlie Walden* played the only first 3 parts 2 times each and did not play the fourth part. *Oscar* and *Doc Harper* played the first part once, the second part twice and parts 3 and 4 one time each as did *Bruce Molsky. Tommy Jackson* and *J.P. Fraley* only played the first two parts, twice each.

You get my drift. SO, the only *rule* here is to agree amongst yourselves how many times to play each of the how many parts you choose to play. It doesn't even have to be the same each time through the tune. NOW you start to understand why old time guitar players have to be mind readers as well!

# Black Hills Waltz
**From the playing of Kenner "KC" Kartchner of Snowflake, AZ**

A tuning
aEAC#E (G tuning capo 2)

Track 5

# Bob Tailed Mule
**From the playing of Kenner "KC" Kartchner of Snowflake, AZ**

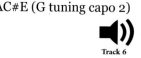

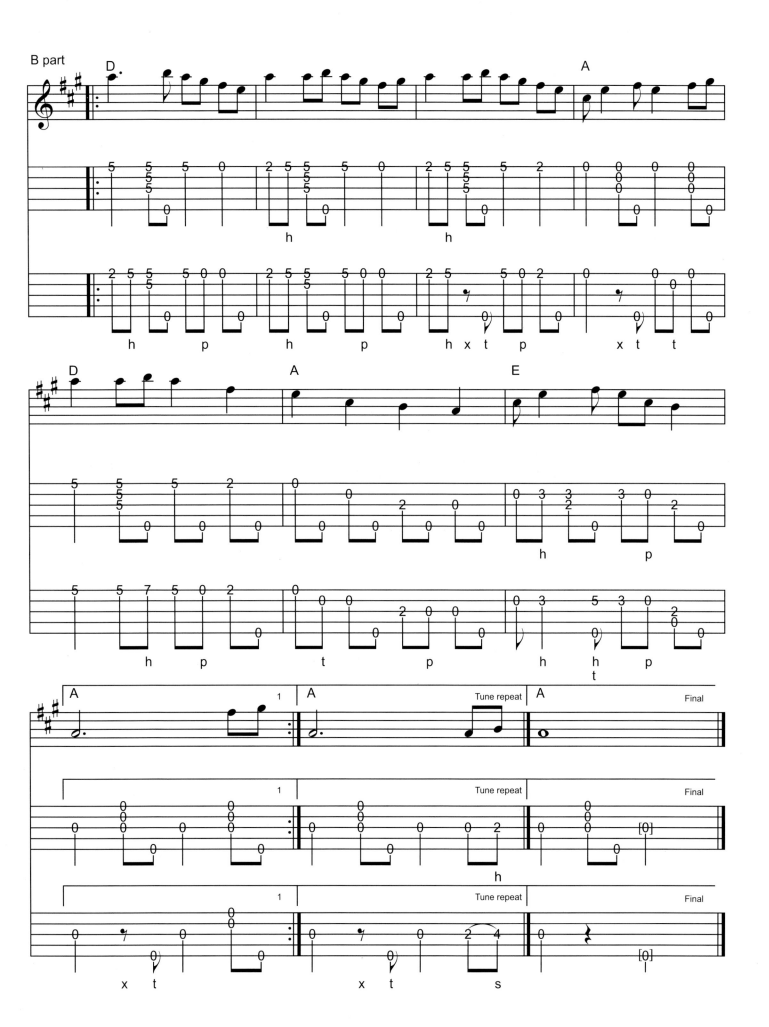

# Bonapart's Retreat
## Wm. H. Stepp version (aka the *Beef* commercial version)

Double D tuning
aDADE (double C capo 2)

Track 7

22

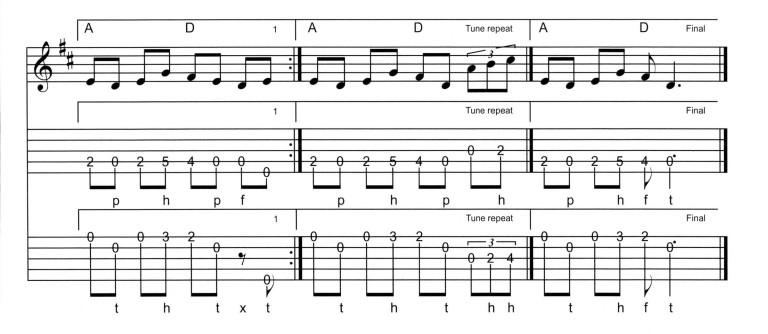

This one is fun and not really too hard. This version is known by many folks both from the *Beef, it's what's for dinner* commercial and more importantly as *Hoe-Down* from Aaron Copland's *Rodeo* (pronounced Ro *DA* O).

What is not as well known is that while Copland composed, copyrighted, then premiered this piece around 1942, the tune had been recorded and collected by Ruth Seeger and the Library of Congress in 1936 as Bonaparte's Retreat played on fiddle by William H. Stepp. Copland took the transcription of Stepp's playing note for note to start his composition.

The original recording is still available today for you to hear for yourself. I love it when you can hear someone say, "And this here's the bony part" right on the recording! Of course, today you may just hear someone say, "Where's the beef?"

Play nice!

# Booth Shot Lincoln

A tuning
aEAC#E (G tuning capo 2)

Track 8

24

Yes! That *is* an F#m in the 4th measure of each part AND as the final chord. I know, many folks consider that too *modern* but that is how I learned it and have always played it. If you don't like that sound or feel, use the D chord instead but be prepared for the discussion either way.

And *yes*, we ended with that chord leaving the final note unresolved which just seems to be the appropriate amount of tension or *cool* factor this tune wants.

# Briar Picker Brown

Double D tuning
aDADE (double C capo 2)

Track 9

26

Yes, there are some hammer ons to unplayed strings. I seem to do it more often than I thought!

# Cluck Old Hen

A *modal* tuning
aEADE (G *modal* tuning capo 2)

Track 10

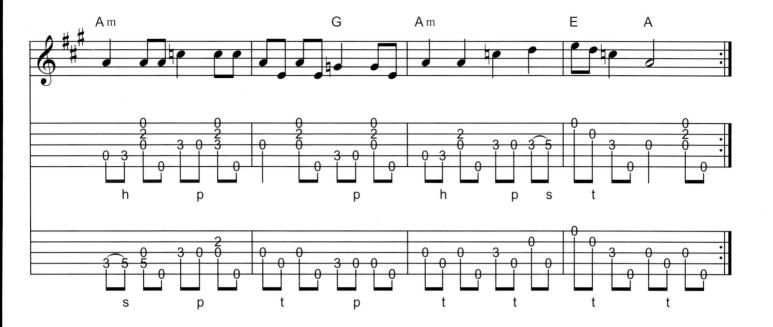

In *modal* tuning the C and G notes are *natural,* not sharped. I've tried to be consistent as I wrote this and keep that rule throughout the writing of this tune. So in the tab there is a recurring 2-3 slide that keeps the rule intact. HOWEVER some folks do this consistently in such a tune, others not.

That means that the 2-3 slide in measure 4 and measure 8 of the advanced A part and the first measure of the advanced B part can be played as a 3-4 slide instead of the 2-3. This changes the character of the tune and also the accompanying chord.

Also, as to chords in this one, I have written them as I feel I would want them played by my accompanist. You may feel different. You may want an *Am* in the first part and prefer to end the tune on an *Am* as well. You may not want as many chord changes in the first part or want more changes in the second. As always, this is entirely up to you and the people you play music with. Enjoy it and play it as you like it.

Just...
    Play Nice!

# Cold Frosty Morning
**Henry Reed and Mel Durham inspired version**

A *modal* tuning
aEADE (G *modal* tuning capo 2)

This version is based upon the tune collected as played by *Henry Reed* and *Mel Durham*. It is in the key that is referred to as *A modal* so your C and G notes are natural instead of sharp as in the key of A major. (Please don't ask me to explain modes of music. There is more than one mode. Get a music theory book if you want to understand this better). This is what gives this tune – and other so called *modal* tunes their minor, dark sound.

You will notice that in the beginning of the B part it starts with an A major chord. Why? Who knows, that is just the way most of the folks I heard play it played it. And, yes, I like the A major chord there. You can choose. Want to keep the *modal* sound all the way through, just use the Am. Like always, that choice remains up to you and the folks you play with.

*Note from a student:* Paul writes, "Just a thought – on the 1st line in the B part, 2nd measure, if you do a short bar across strings 1&2 when you land on the A note (1st string 5th fret) then you can play the G (3rd fret) with the thumb without having to slide. Then the hand lifts and moves back to first position to get ready for measure 3. Again just a thought…"

# Cold Frosty Morning
## This version is the one played by Melvin Wine

# The Cuckoo

G *modal* tuning
gDGCD

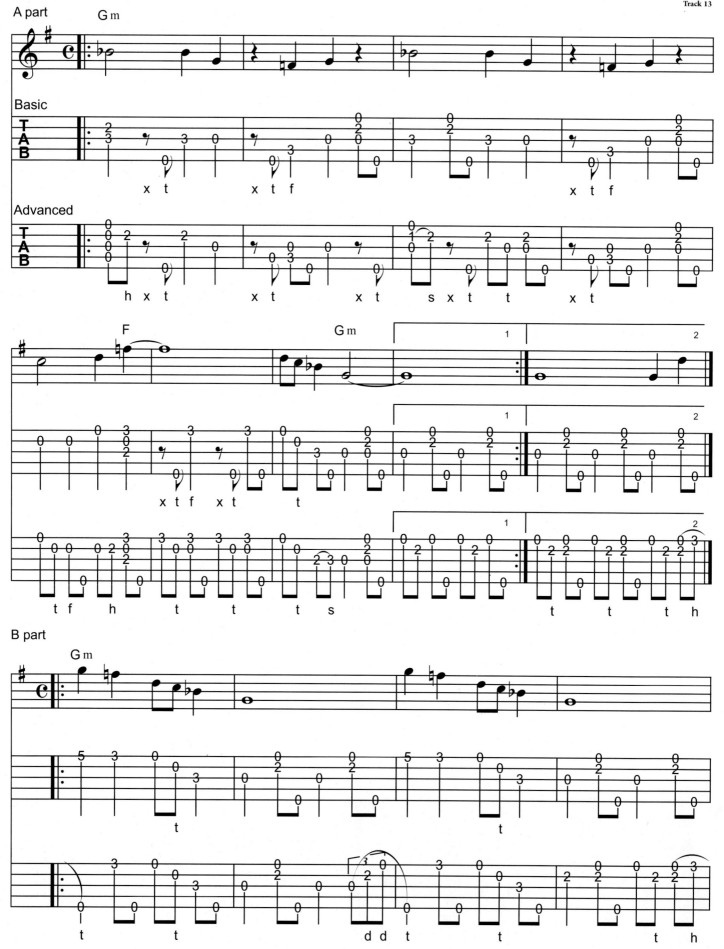

34

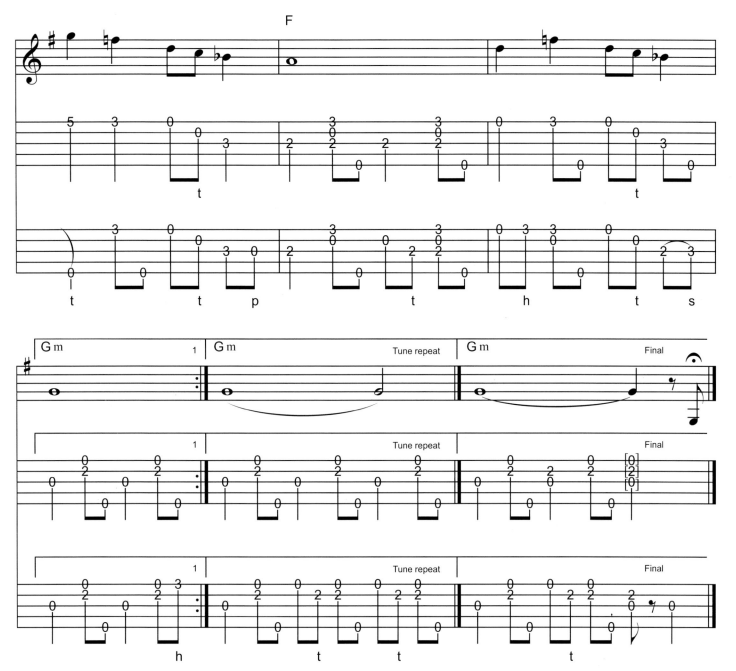

There are SO many variations on this tune both notational and timing-wise that while this should get you started, you will really want to pick a version that you and your friends agree on.

As it is here, yes, there are 6 beats in the 2nd endings of both parts and the final ending.

AND just to confuse matters a bit more, for one more variation, the extra three measures below can replace measures 1 and 2 in the B part AND replace measures 3 & 4 as well making the first 4 measures of the B part 6 measures long for a total of a 10 measure B part. Phew! Enjoy...

*Alternate for B measures 1 & 2 (and 3 & 4) - these 3 measures take the place of each pair.*

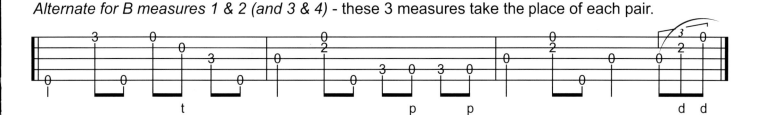

# Cumberland Gap

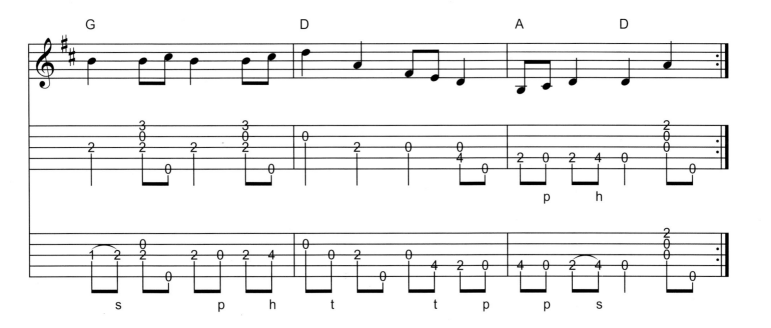

This is a three part version I learned in the mid 80's at the Mount Airy Festival. I believe I got it from Thorn Carey who lived in North Carolina at the time.

It is the B part that is the additional or third part of this tune. Many play the A and C parts for a complete – and square – tune. I like the three-part variation.

# Doctor Doctor

Double D tuning
aDADE (double C capo 2)

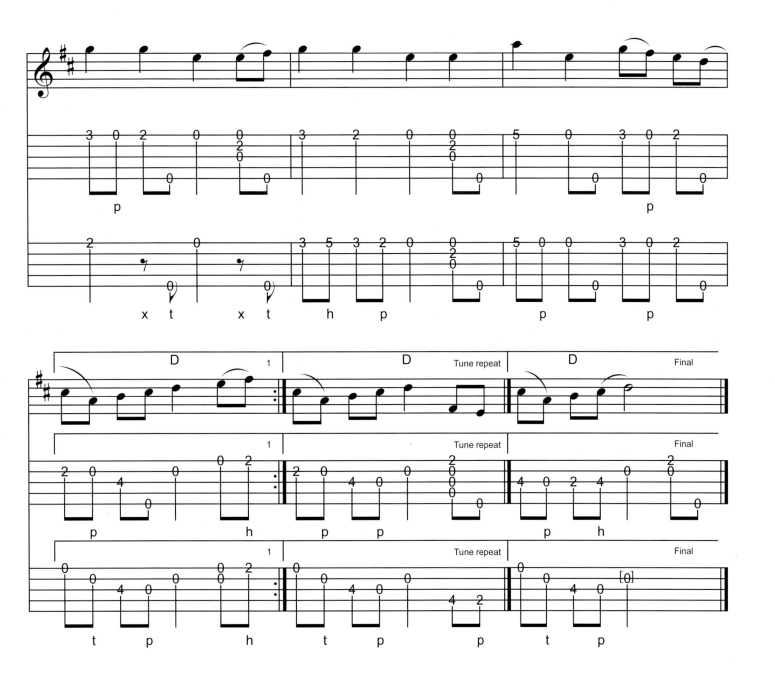

# Duck River

Double D tuning
aDADE (double C capo 2)
Track 16

40

# Ducks on the Millpond

Double D tuning
aDADE (double C capo 2)

Track 17

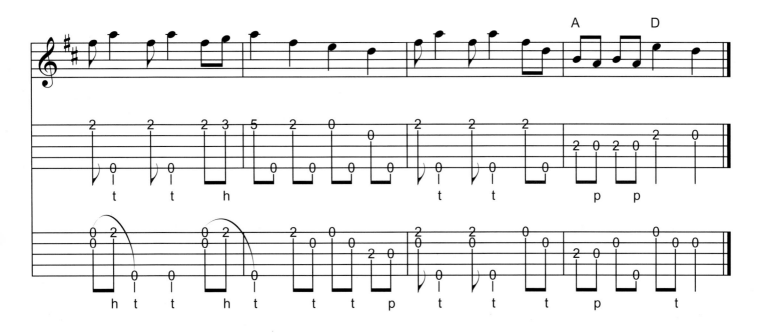

# Ebenezer

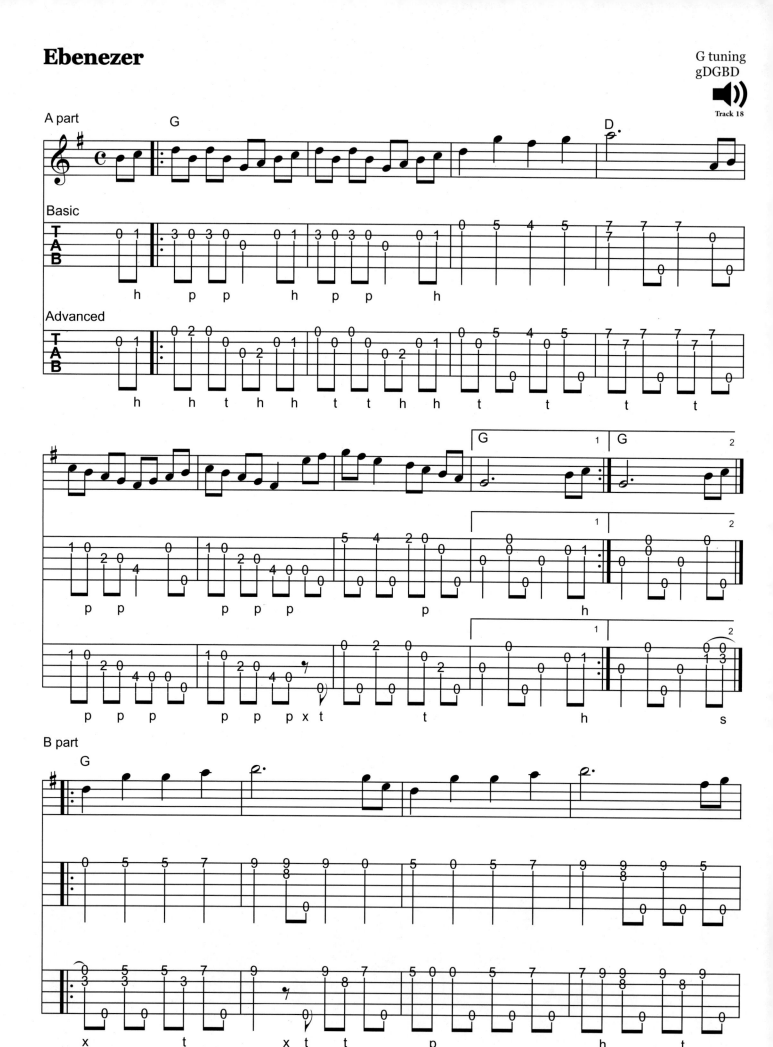

44

# Mr. Fishar's Hornpipe - 3 part version
## aka Fisher's Hornpipe

Double D tuning
aDADE (double C capo 2)
Track 19

C part

47

# Folding Down the Sheets

48

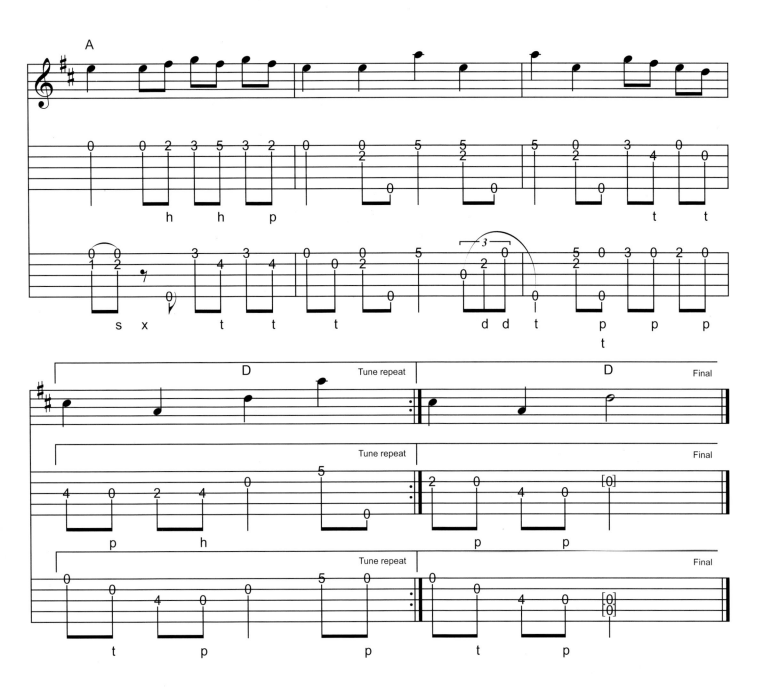

# Forked Deer

Double D tuning
aDADE (double C capo 2)

Track 21

50

# Fortune

Double D tuning
aDADE (double C capo 2)

Track 22

# Great Big Taters in a Sandy Land

G tuning
gDGBD

Track 23

Texas fiddle greats *Eck Robertson* and *Lewis Thomasson* both play this in *G*. These days, many folks play it in *A*. It works well on the fiddle in both keys so banjo players just have to play the same notes in the same tuning but in the right key. And we all know it is usually the fiddler who decides which key. Capo or tune up, it's up to you.

When *Eck* was recorded, he started with a B part but does play the parts in the order written here ending with the C part. *Lewis Thomasson* likewise starts on B and then plays through.

I've written it *crooked* with two extra measures in the A part. *W. E. Claunch* with *Christine Haygood* play it that way on the *Great Big Yam Potatoes* recording as do *Lisa Ornstein* with *Andy Cahan* and *Laura Fishleder* on their landmark recording *Ship in the Clouds* which is probably where I first heard this tune.

Find any or all of these recordings to get a feel for how it was played by the greats. Like all old time, everyone plays it different. That is just how they did it, so you get to choose how you are going to play it. Just make sure y'all agree before you start or at least be ready to adjust as you go.

Notes on the Tab: Those *x*'s under tied notes mean that you don't strike the note again, you just let those notes ring on until the next struck note.

# Grey Eagle

A tuning
aEAC#E (G tuning capo 2)

Track 24

56

# Johnson Boys

Double D tuning
aDADE (double C capo 2)

Track 25

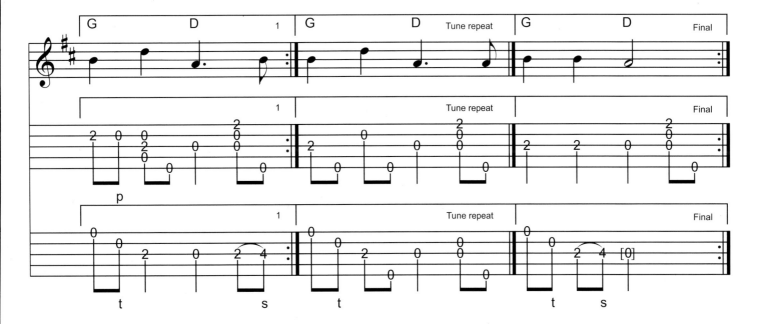

Have you heard the many a story
told by old and young with joy
Of the many deeds a daring
that was done by the Johnson boys

Jump up pretty girls don't be afraid, Jump up pretty girls don't be afraid
Jump up pretty girls don't be afraid, Jump up pretty girls don't be afraid

Johnson boys, they're the fellers
they know how to court them girls
They know how to hug and a'kiss 'em
jump up pretty girls don't be afraid

Jump up pretty girls don't be afraid, Jump up pretty girls don't be afraid
Jump up pretty girls don't be afraid, Jump up pretty girls don't be afraid

They were men of skill and courage
and they traveled near and far
And they joined the country service
in that awful Civil War

Jump up pretty girls don't be afraid, Jump up pretty girls don't be afraid
Jump up pretty girls don't be afraid, Jump up pretty girls don't be afraid

They were scouts in the Rebel army
and they traveled far and wide
When the Yankees seen them a'comin'
they throwed down their guns & hide

Jump up pretty girls don't be afraid, Jump up pretty girls don't be afraid
Jump up pretty girls don't be afraid, Jump up pretty girls don't be afraid

# Katy Hill

60

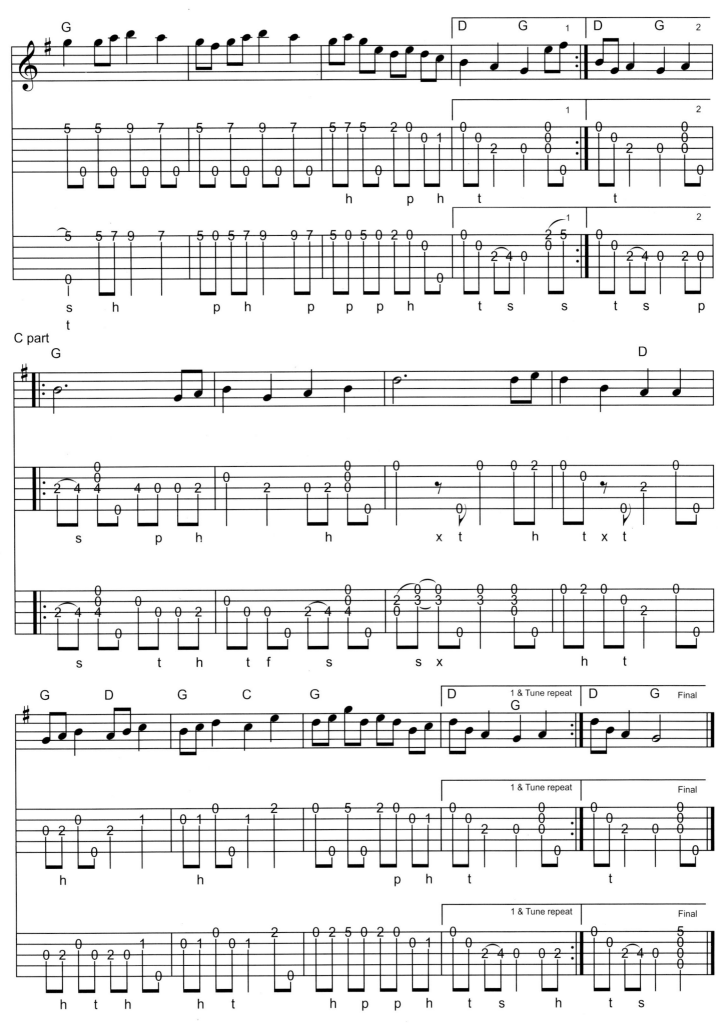

C part

61

# Little Dutch Girl

A tuning
aEAC#E (G capo 2)

Track 27

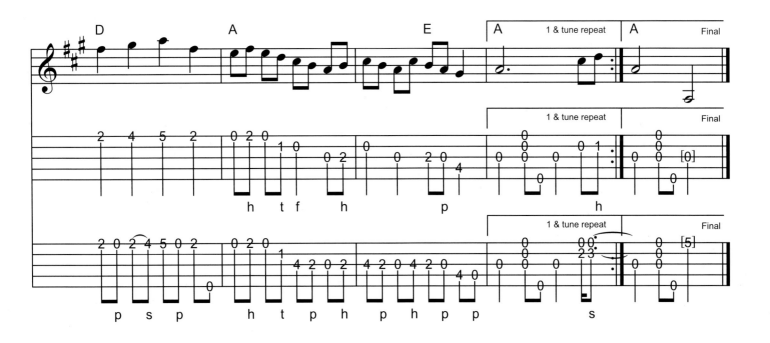

# The Merry Blacksmith
## Gene Goforth calls this *Eminence Breakdown*

Double D tuning
aDADE (double C capo 2)

Track 28

64

# Mississippi Sawyer

Double D tuning
aDADE (double C capo 2)

Track 29

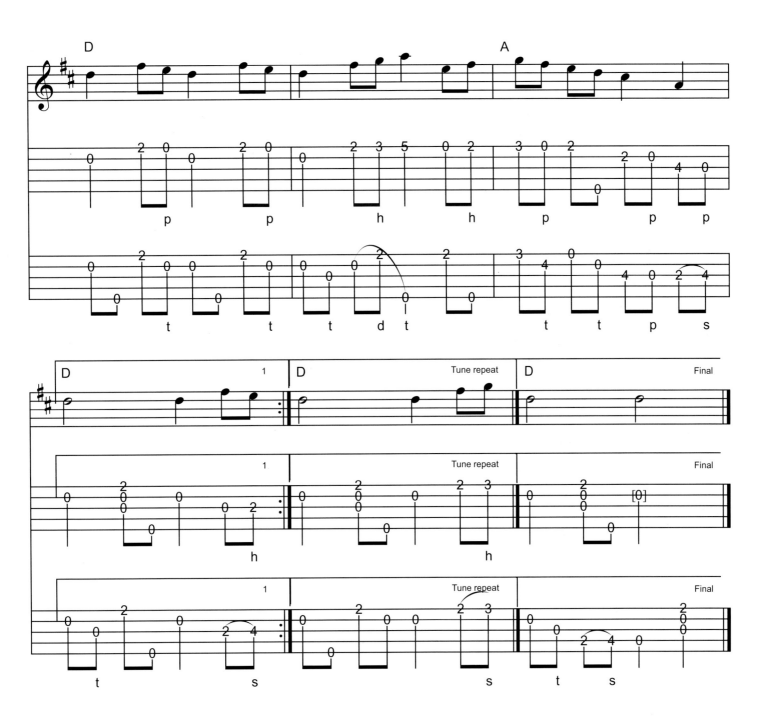

# Roy Wooliver's Money Musk

A tuning
aEAC#E (G capo 2)

Track 30

Alternate C part

# Needlecase

Double D tuning
aDADE (double C capo 2)

Track 31

# Old Belle Cow

A tuning
aEAC#E (G tuning capo 2)

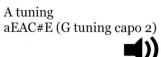
Track 32

72

If you are uncomfortable with the *modal* nature of the B part, or your community plays it *major* instead, just take the 3rd fret on the 4th string (G natural) and make it a 4th fret (G sharp) and use an E chord instead of the G.

I have always heard it the way I have written it and much prefer the sound. Adds tension!

MOOOOooooooo...ving right along.

# Opera Reel

74

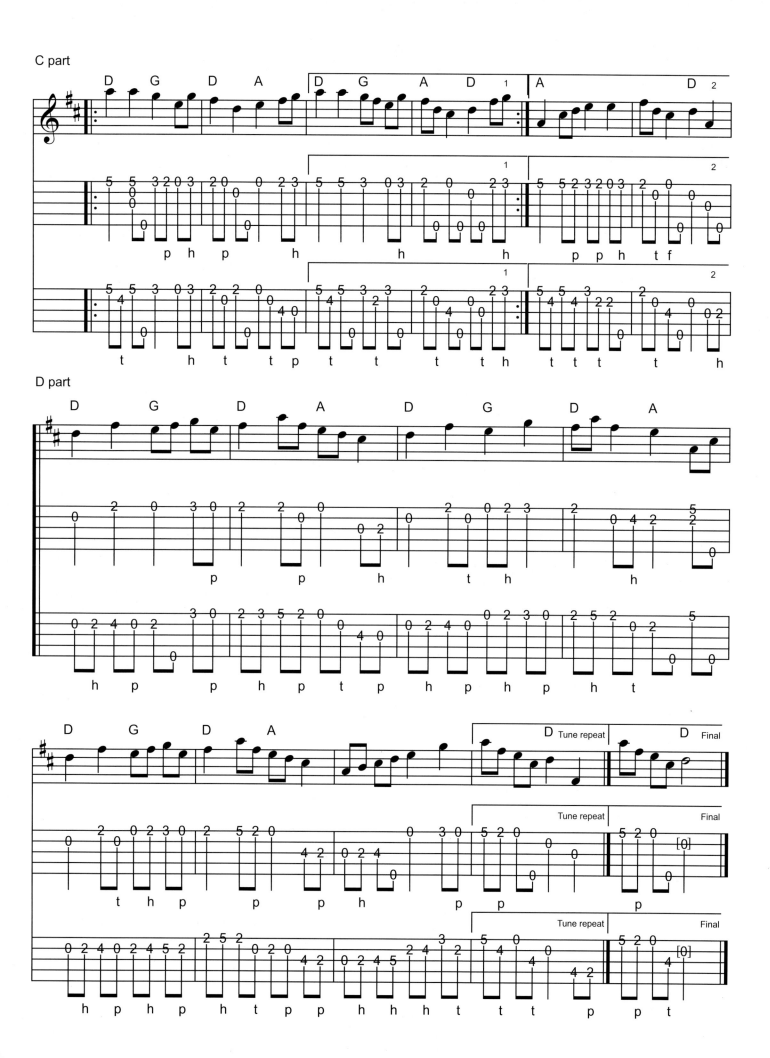

# Over the Waterfall

Double D tuning
aDADE (double C capo 2)

Track 34

76

# Policeman

A tuning
aEAC#E (G tuning capo 2)

Track 35

# Policeman

Police come, I didn't want to go this morning (2x)
Police come, I didn't want to go
Shot him in the head with my 44 this morning

Two little children lying in the bed this morning (2x)
Two little children lying in the bed
One rolled over to the other and said, "it's morning"

I know something I ain gonna tell this morning  (2x)
I know something I ain'a gonna tell
Want to go to heaven in a coconut shell this morning

Bullfrog jumped from bank to bank, this morning (2x)
Bullfrog jumped from bank to bank
Skinned his whole back from shank to shank, this morning.

Great big fellow laying on a log this morning (2x)
Great big fellow laying on a log
Finger on the trigger and his eye on a hog, this morning

Down went the trigger and bang went the gun this morning (2x)
Down went the trigger and bang went the gun
Wish I had a wagon to haul him home, this morning.

# Polly Put the Kettle On

Double D tuning<br>aDADE (double C capo 2)<br>Track 36

C part

81

# Push the Pig's Foot a Little Further Into the Fire

G tuning
gDGBD

Track 37

82

# The Rattlesnake
**from the playing of Kenner "KC" Kartchner of Snowflake, AZ**

A tuning
aEAC#E (G tuning capo 2)

Track 38

This is a beautifully simple tune that has some wonderful subtle twists to the playing of it on the banjo. The advanced line of the banjo tab basically follows the advanced line of the fiddle version though the melodic structure is much the same as the basic line for both instruments.

***Kenner "KC" Kartchner*** was born in Snowflake, AZ, on October 15, 1886 and spent his life and career playing the fiddle for dances and performances throughout the northeastern part of AZ and into New Mexico. He was already quite an accomplished fiddler when Arizona became a state. *KC* passed away in 1970 but his music lives on as a wonderful tie to the past and a great example of fiddle playing of the last centuries.

For more about Kenner C. Kartchner please read his autobiography *Frontier Fiddler – The Life of a Northern Arizona Pioneer* (University of Arizona Press © 1990) edited by Larry V. Shumway who is Kenner's son in law.

# Rock the Cradle Joe

Double D tuning
aDADE (double C capo 2)

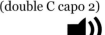

Track 39

86

This is one of the tunes that has gone through some changes since it was first collected by Miles Krassen, which is why you may notice some major differences between the basic and advanced version.

This is seen most significantly in the 1st and 3rd full measures of the A part and the 3rd measure of the B part where you jump up to the high *B* note (7th fret on the first string). The melody will be interchangeable to the basic one (the one most folks recognize), but you will notice that a *G chord* is more appropriate at that point in the tune and will sound better to most people than the D chord, as in the basic version. That is why I wrote another suggested chord line as presented on the advanced part.

# Sally's Got Mud Between Her Toes
### aka Sal's Got Mud Between Her Toes

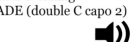

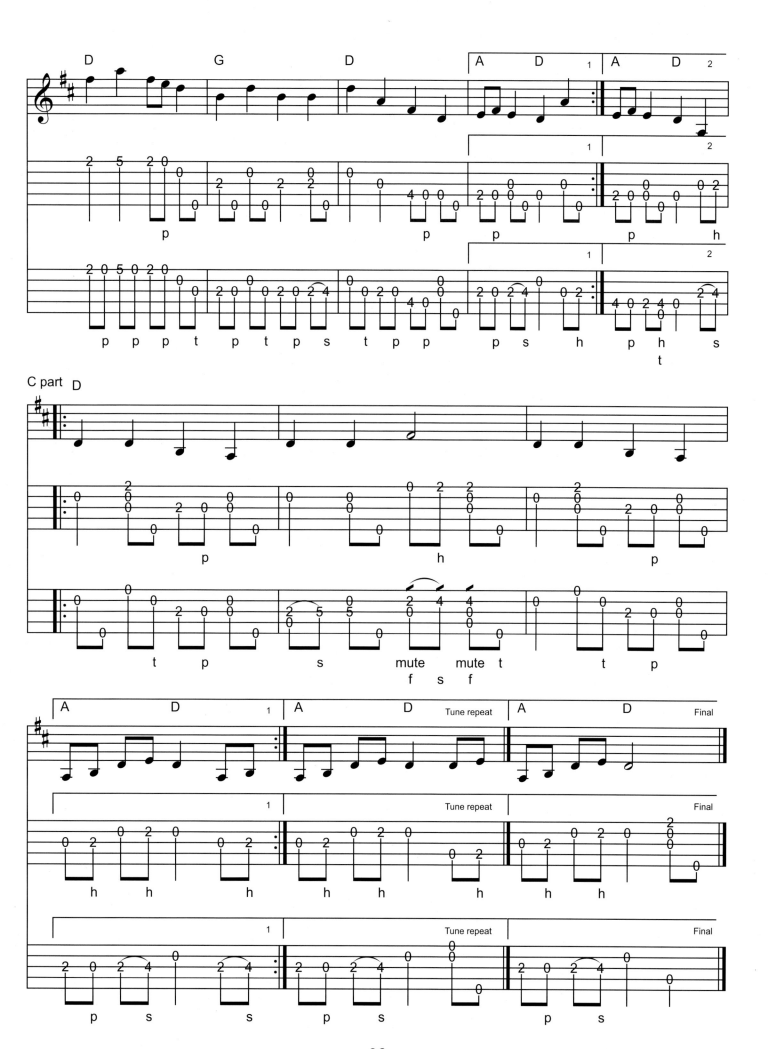

C part

# Salt Creek
## aka Salt River

# Salty River Reel

A tuning
aEAC#E (G tuning capo 2)

Track 42

# Shady Grove
## Modal version

Track 43

94

# Doc Robert's Shortnin' Bread
**Not your mama's little baby's shortnin' bread!**

G tuning
gDGBD

Track 44

96

C part

Continues on next page

97

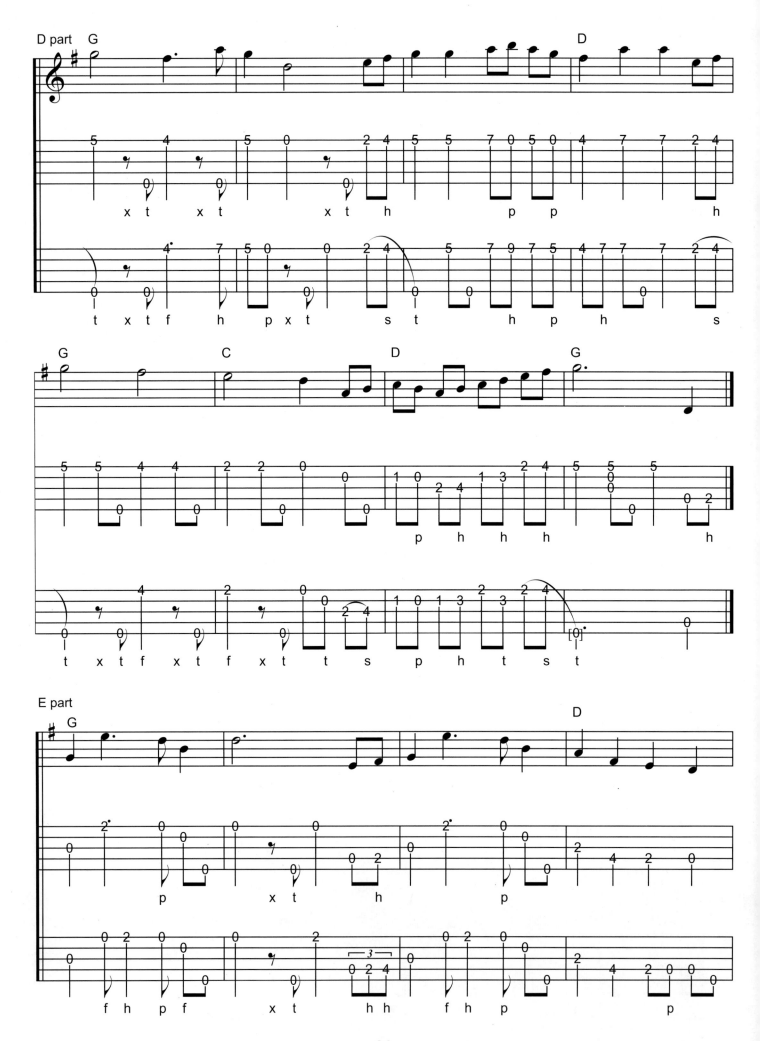

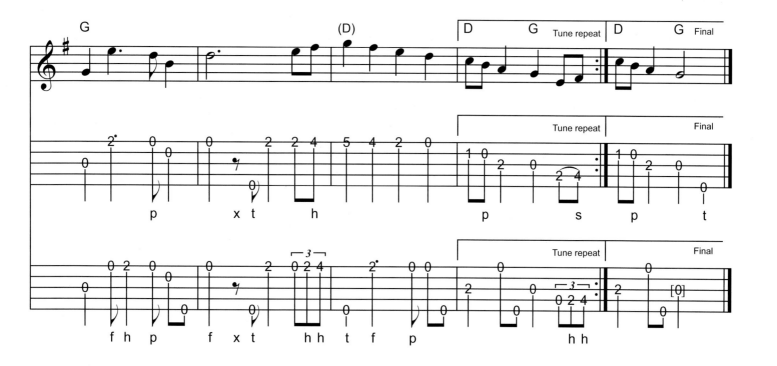

Sorry this one goes over so many pages. The number of parts (5!) makes it necessary.

Okay, banjo players. Enjoy this one. Lots of syncopation and interesting runs here. Hammers, pulls, slides and more! Galax licks galore! Don't say this one is just the same ol dum did dy tune.

5 parts and only one of them repeats! Some may consider the parts I have marked as C and D to be variants of the same part but to me there were enough differences in how *Doc Roberts* played them for me to decide to write them separately.

*Doc's* playing of this one is so truly wonderful that I would strongly urge you to make sure you find and listen to his recording of it to hear all the variation and strength in his playing.

In many cases banjo playing is more *interpretive* than literal and this tune shows that throughout. Just like in the fiddle version, this transcription really only gives you a start on learning to play this tune. It's like I always say, *Listen, listen, listen!* Each time I listen to *Doc* play it I hear more and more. To me it's as much about the musical journey as the final tune.

BTW, as far as listening, notice the D chord in parenthesis at the next to last measure of the tune. I sometimes like to put it in here - a bit early to some - but it isn't necessary to have the chord at that spot so *LISTEN* and decide what sounds best to you.

# Snowbird

100

# Soldier's Joy

Double D tuning
aDADE (double C capo 2)

Track 46

102

# Spotted Pony
## aka Snowshoes

I know, I know. Most of you folks who started with my Clawhammer Banjo From Scratch book have most likely had enough of this one. BUT, I hope there is enough variation here to make you enjoy it again.

# Step Around Johnny

Double D tuning
aDADE (double C capo 2)

Track 48

# Sugar Hill

Double D tuning
aDADE (double C capo 2)

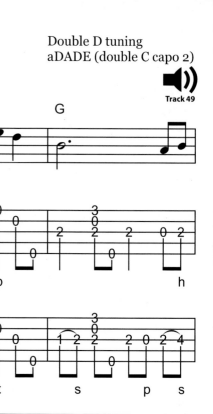

Track 49

A part

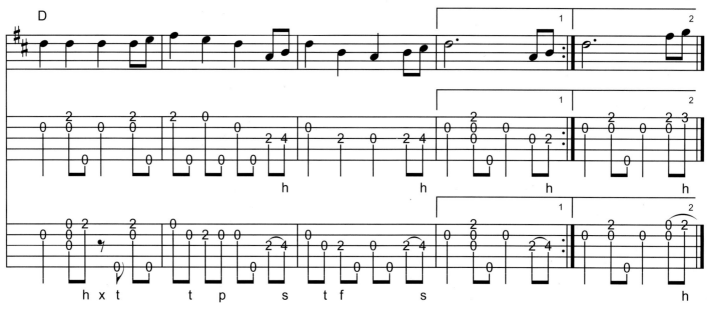

B part

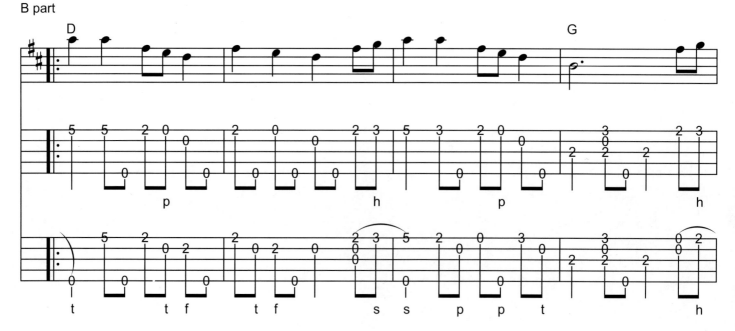

108

Some folks reverse these parts but I play it this way because the melody goes verse, chorus.

If you want to get your eye knocked out
If you want to get a thrill
If you want to get your head stomped in
Go up on Sugar Hill...

And YES! You did notice that the second part sounds a LOT like the second part of
Angelina Baker... But then don't they ... never mind. Not going there.

# Three Thin Dimes

C part

# Three Way Hornpipe

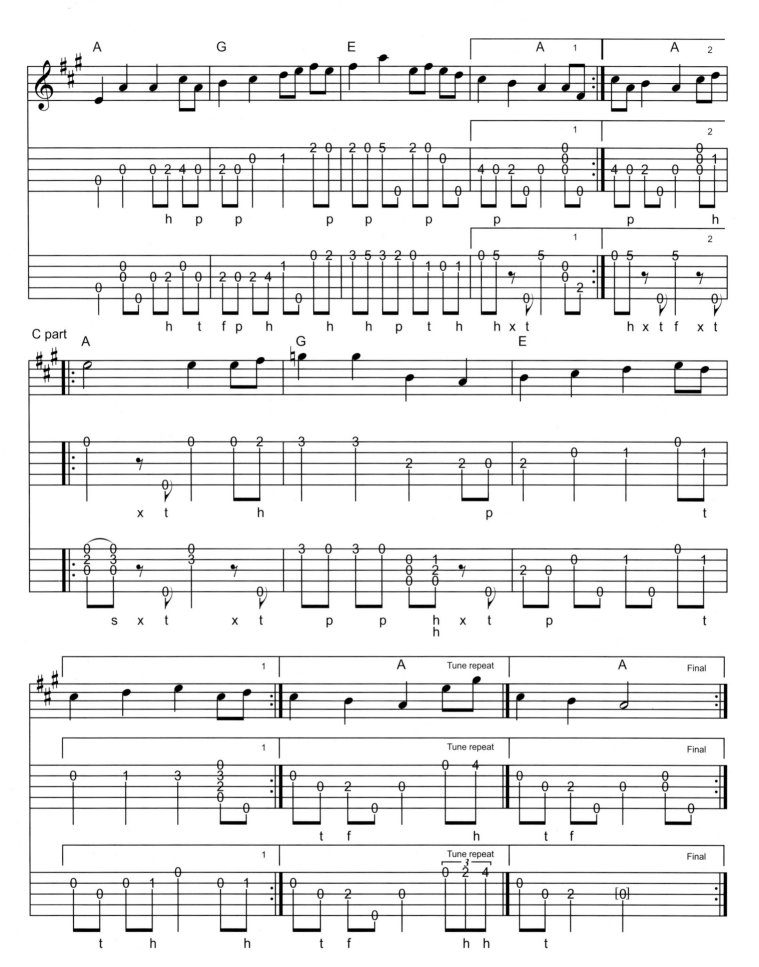

You will notice some conflicts in the B part. I'd recommend getting Joe Sharp & Band's recording from *Traditional Music of the Cumberland Plateau vol. 2* (Originally County 787). They have lots more notes and variation in their playing of it and while it's my *source* I have made it my own in several ways.

# Waiting for the Federals
## aka Seneca Square Dance

G tuning
gDGBD

Track 52

114

Many folks don't use and/or don't care for the Em in the third full measure of the A part. I happen to love it and in the fiddle playing will chord the fiddle to match, in essence asking my guitar and banjo players to put it in.

Likewise, you can use it in the 3rd measure of the B part even though I didn't write it there.

As always, it is up to you to choose what you like to hear and play. Just make sure you and your fiddler agree.

# Walk Along John To Kansas

A tuning
aEAC#E (G tuning capo 2)

Track 53

B part

116

This is another of Kenner "KC" Kartchner's tunes. KC was a wonderful fiddler from northeastern Arizona who was born in the late 1800's and living and playing well into the 20th century.

And YES, there are 10 measures in the B part.

# Walking in the Parlor

Double D tuning
aDADE (double C capo 2)

Track 54

# West Fork Gals

120

# Whitesburg

A tuning
aEAC#E (G tuning capo 2)

Track 56

122

This tune is wonderfully circular in that it seems like it starts again before it even really ends.

Note that in the first full measure of the tune on the advanced line, the 5th fret on the first string is in parentheses ( ) to tell you not to try to play it (that 5th fret note) in the first pass of the tune. However, when you come back into the first part from the repeat ending you are coming in from a fretted chord figure (4th fret on the first string, 3rd fret on the second), which I like to play with my first and second fingers. This allows you to just put your *third* finger down onto the 5th fret on the first string to start the tune again. You play that note *INSTEAD* of the open fifth string (still an *A* note) with a *down* stroke so the finger plays the note instead of the thumb.

You can replace the last two notes of the *Tune repeat* ending with the open 1st string to 2nd fret hammer on (as in the pick-up measure or the 2-4-5 slide up WITH the thumb playing the open fifth string as in measures 4 & 5 of the advanced A part. Your choice. Have fun with it and know that once you get the flow, it will just perk along over and over until you finally decide to end the tune. That is when you'll need that final note or extra measure you see at the end of the tune. Enjoy!

123

# (There is a) Wild Hog in the Woods

Double D tuning
aDADE (double C capo 2)

Track 57

124

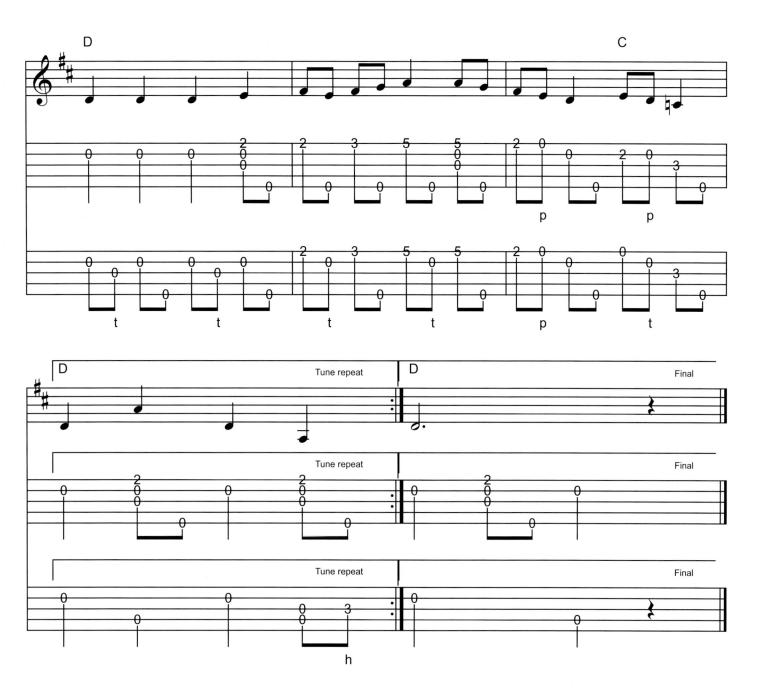

Yes, this is what is often referred to as a *modal* tune (no, we are not discussing modes and/or which one) but notice that I do not use *modal tuning* for it.

There was an interesting discussion of this topic years ago in *Banjo Newsletter Magazine*. One author said *modal* tunings were "a must" while in the same issue another author said he didn't know "why folks bother with modal tunings" as he felt that they were just unnecessary. You get to choose in the long run, but this tune shows that *modal* tuning is not a *must* in order to get a *modal sound* in tunes.

# Wild Horses at Stony Point

A part (or A-1 and no repeat if you use the alternative A-2.)

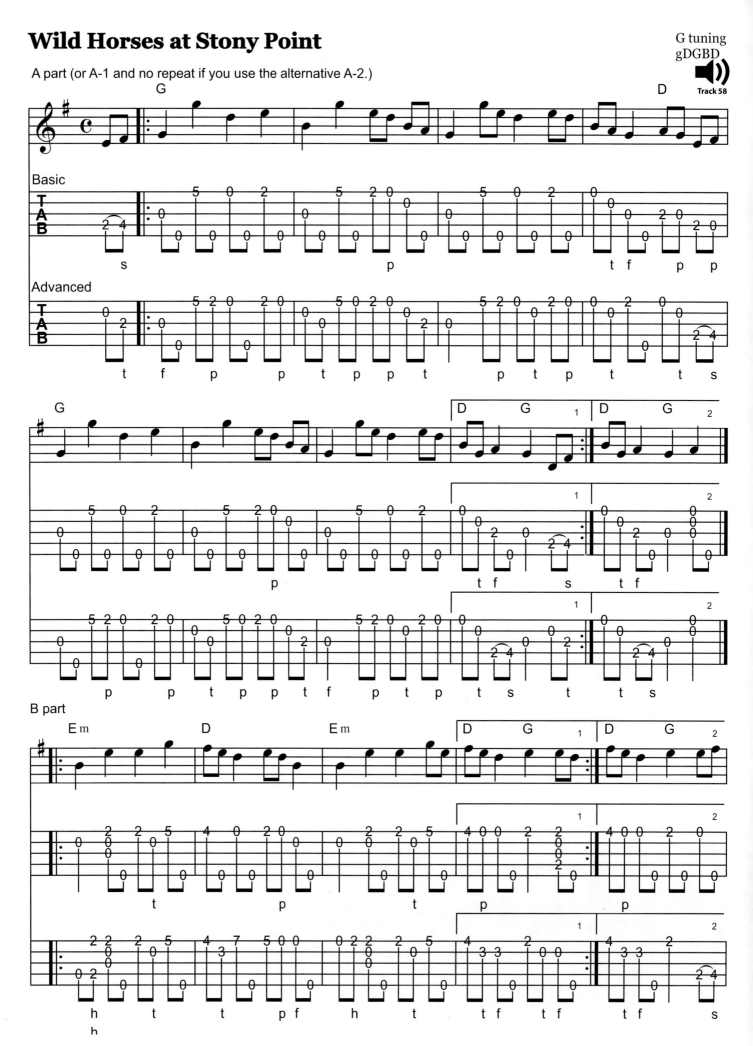

126

C part

Alternate A - 2. Many folks like to play this as the second A part. Playing this with the repeat makes 1 complete part.

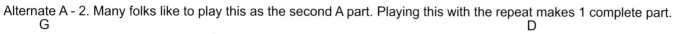

127

# Wooden Nickel
**by Mark Gapponoff - used with permission**

Double D tuning
aDADE (double C capo 2)

Track 59

128

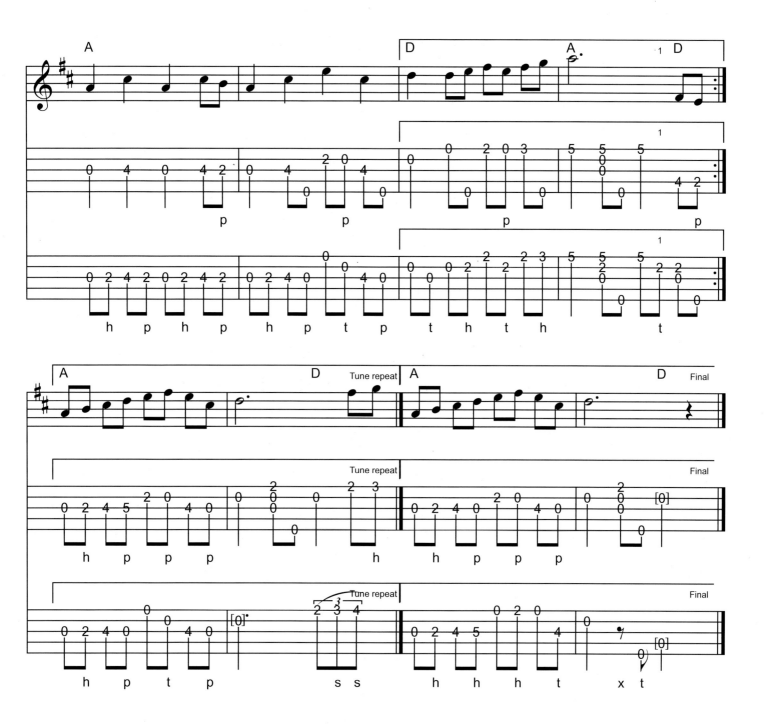

Mark Gapponoff wrote this wonderful tune which my band, *The Boiled Buzzards,* recorded on our CD *Early Bird Special* (Buzzard 1004 CD) which as of this writing is still available as CD and download.

This one can be a great place to practice your fingering gymnastics and *one finger one fret* reaches as it kind of goes all over the place. Notice especially the third measure in the advanced B part where your pinky is on the 5th fret of the fourth string as your index has to do pull offs from the second fret to the open 3rd string!

*Hammers and pulls and thumbs! Oh MY!*

# Year of Jubilo
## aka Lincoln's Gunboats

Double D tuning
aDADE (double C capo 2)

# Yellow Barber

Double D tuning
aDADE (double C capo 2)

Track 61

132

# Y. Z. Hamilton's Special Breakdown

G tuning
gDGBD

B part

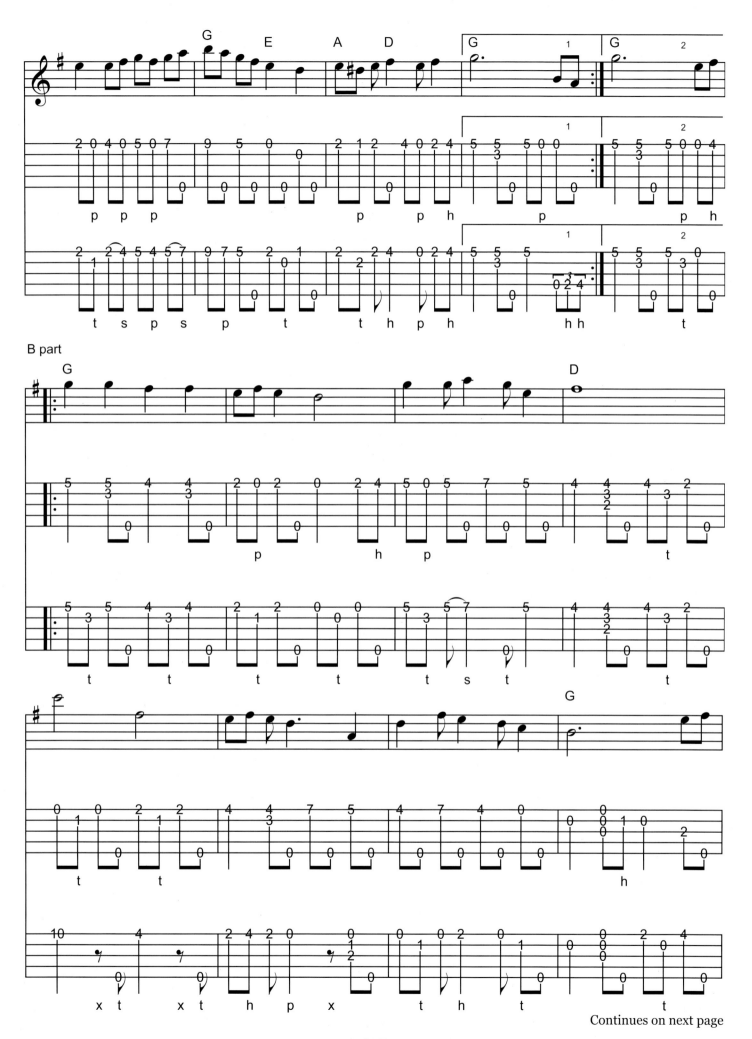

Continues on next page

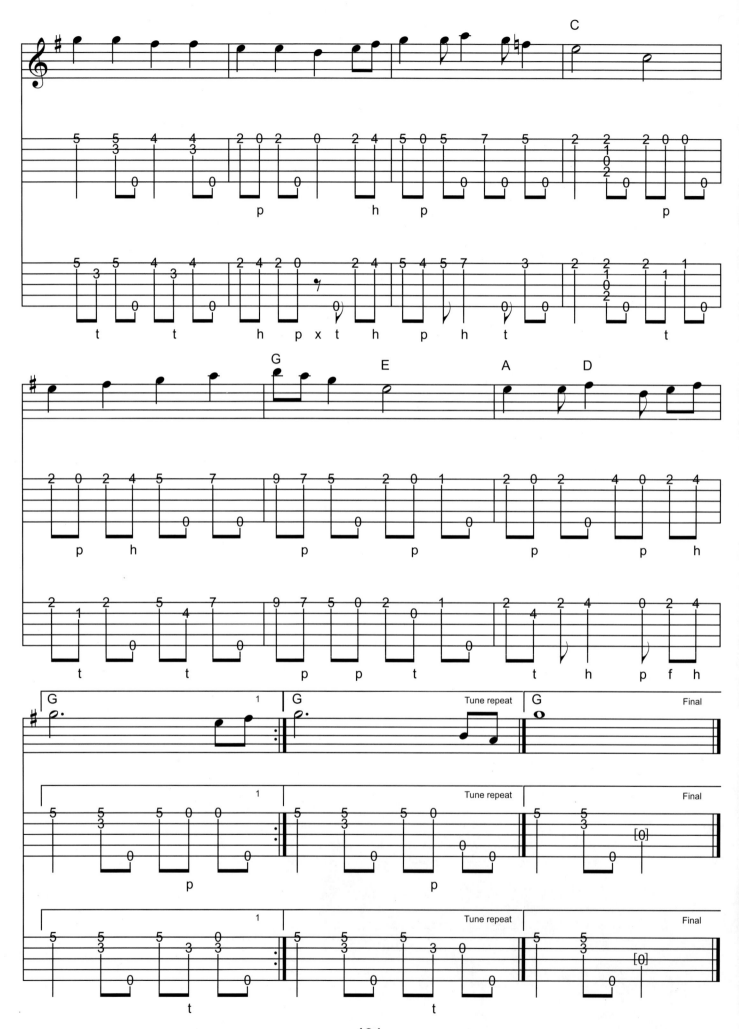

# About Y.Z. Hamilton

Born: Randolph Co., AL

"Often identified as state fiddle champion of Alabama by virtue of a large convention he won in Birmingham in 1925. There he overcame such well-known fiddlers as A.A. Gray, Earl Johnson, and Charlie Stripling. He recorded "Hamilton's Special Breakdown" (ed. - Paramount 33186) and "Fifty Years Ago" for Paramount in 1926. In 1927 "Old Sefus Brown" and "Because He Was Only a Tramp" for Gennett. He also fiddled with a popular Birmingham band, Uncle Bud and His Boll Weevils, which regularly played on the radio, did school house performances, and entered fiddlers' conventions."

Source: Alabama Music Hall of Fame

http://www.alabamamusicoffice.com/artists-a-z/h/944-hamilton-yz

# About the Tune

AKA *Y. Z. Hamilton's Breakdown* or simply *Hamilton's Breakdown*. This tune was originally recorded in 1926 by Y. Z. Hamilton and his recording of it is available today on the compilation album *Possum Up A Gum Stump* which is a collection of Alabama tunes and is still available as of this writing from the Alabama Music Office listed above. I keep rediscovering this tune and a few summers ago I finally decided to learn to play it. I love that it is not as straight forward as many old time tunes have become, but quite a little diddy! I strongly urge you to listen to YZ's recording of this tune. He really gets a lot out of it and way more than I could show in one or two passes of the tune.

There is a session tape of the *Canote Brothers* playing and teaching this tune from a repertoire class which is where I first heard the tune. I was quite captivated with it even then and touched upon it over the years. However, hearing YZ play it (discovering it on my iTunes list once I could search tunes by title) it seems the *Canotes* demonstrated only one of the several variants of the B part that YZ plays so it is only by listening to YZ's playing that you will get the full flavor of this tune.

Since I now spend so much time playing with the *Old Time Fiddlers Association* crowd - indeed I was president of the Yuma, AZ chapter for several years - I felt it could fit right in. My guitar player out here - Dennis *drypitstop* Russell took right to it and we even used it as a teaching tune at one of our monthly *Fiddle Jam Workshops*. The group got it pretty quick and it has become a favorite of Yuma's Territorial chapter of the Arizona Old Time Fiddlers Association. Find out more about that chapter and more about our *Jam Workshops* at *www. YumaOldTimeFiddlers.com* and come play with them if you are out that way.

Those astute listeners among you may recognize the opening phrases of *Whistling Rufus* at the beginning of the tune. That's another good one, and if you are interested, you can find a transcription of it in my book *Old Time Festival Tunes for Clawhammer Banjo* (MB 20313).

You can find more information on this tune at http://www.fiddlehangout.com/topic/17508

*Possum Up A Gum Stump* can be ordered as a CD at http://www.alabamafolklife.org/content/possum-gum-stump-home-field-and-commercial-recordings-alabama-fiddlers

# Other products by Dan Levenson

## Books

***Clawhammer Banjo From Scratch*** - (MB 20190BCD ) - This book starts at the beginning. 12 common jam session tunes are presented in double thumb and drop thumb technique. Includes 2 CDs.

***Fiddle From Scratch*** (MB 22256) This book and accompanying 2 CDs are an excellent introduction to the fiddle and old time music. This book starts at the beginning. 12 common jam session tunes are presented, from basic melodies to full blown jam versions. 3 additional tunes are also included to get you into other keys. It even introduces you to *cross tuning* - an important old time technique.

***First Lessons Folk Banjo*** (MB 22257 BCD) - Banjo tablature with companion CD. This one will teach you to play the banjo as a folk instrument to back up your singing, strum along with others, and even play the whole tune. Both down–picking and up–picking banjo styles are presented here so you have a choice on how to play even if you never played any instrument.

***First Lessons Clawhammer Banjo*** (MB 22258 BCD) - Banjo tablature with companion CD. Starting from the beginning with banjo basics and how to read banjo music called tablature, moving quickly into technique, this one will get you started. Beginning in G tuning and introducing others, you can start here and quickly be able to play clawhammer style, even if you never played any instrument at all.

***Old Time Festival Tunes for Clawhammer Banjo*** (MB 20313 BCD) - Tablature with Standard Notation and 2 companion CDs - Mel Bay Publications 117 Old Time favorites with basic and advanced tab plus a standard notation line for other instruments.

***Old Time Festival Tunes for Fiddle & Mandolin*** (MB 21023 BCD)- Tablature with Standard Notation and 2 companion CDs - Mel Bay Publications 117 Old Time favorites with basic and advanced standard notation plus a tab line for mandolin and fiddle.

***Wade Ward - Clawhammer Master*** (MB 22243 BCD) - Banjo tablature with companion CD Tunes of clawhammer master Wade Ward co-written with Bob Carlin. Two tabs of each of 28 tunes both as the master played them and as they are often interpreted today.

***Kyle Creed - Clawhammer Master*** (MB 22137 BCD) - Banjo tablature with companion CD. Tunes of clawhammer master Kyle Creed co-written with Bob Carlin. Two tabs of each of 28 tunes both as the master played them and as they are often interpreted today.

***Buzzard Banjo Clawhammer Style*** (MB 99126BCD) - Tab book with companion CD. 25 tunes tabbed out as played by Dan Levenson with companion CD of the tabs. Includes some basic instruction.

***Gospel Tunes for Clawhammer Banjo*** (MB 21432 BCD) - Tablature with Standard Notation and companion CD - Mel Bay Publications - 27 Favorite Gospel tunes in an easy to play format.

**DVDs** - ***Clawhammer Banjo From Scratch*** - DVD set (MB 5003 DVD) - Instructional video - Clawhammer banjo players, start here! Disc 1 teaches the basics *From Scratch* through the double thumb *Spotted Pony* in double C. Disc 2 tunes you up to Double D and then picks up and adds drop thumb, hammer-ons, pull-offs, more.

## Recordings

***Traveling Home*** (Buzzard 2005 CD) - Banjo, fiddle, guitar and song solos and duos with Dan, Miss Jennifer and Rick Barron. Tunes: *Red Haired Boy; Leaving Home; John Brown's Dream; Dry & Dusty; Camp Chase/ Jenny Git Around; Texas Gals; John Lover's Gone; Texas; Milwaukee Blues; Kentucky John Henry; Lost Indian; Boatman; Durang's Hornpipe; Monkey on a Dogcart; Whistling Rufus; Sandy Boys; Arkansas Traveler/Mississippi Sawyer/Rock the Cradle Joe; Banjo Tramp.*

**Barenaked Banjos** (Buzzard 2002 CD) - 24 all solo banjo pieces. 4 different banjos! Tunes: *Katy Hill; Logan County Blues; Little Billie Wilson; Dr. Dr.; Texas Gals; Forked Deer; Staten Island; Liza Poor Gal; Johnny Don't Get Drunk; Rocky Pallet; Needlecase; Old Bell Cow; Fortune; Old Molly Hare/Rag Time Annie; Soldier's Joy; Billy in the Low Ground; Joke on the Puppy; Breaking Up Christmas; Whiskey Before Breakfast; Hangman's Reel; Duck River; Flying Indian; June Apple; Wild Horses at Stoney Point.*

**Light of the Moon** (Buzzard 2001 CD) - Fiddle tunes to folk songs are what you will find in this recording. Dan is joined on a few songs with other musicians including Annie Trimble of the Boiled Buzzards, and his son Jonathan. Tunes: *June Apple; Cindy; Rushing the Pepper; Climbing the Golden Stairs; All God's Critters; Jaybird/Moses Hoe the Corn; Old Rip; The Fox; Rockin' Jenny; Soppin' the Gravy; Willow Waltz; Darlin' Corey; Buffalo Gals; Yellow Rose of Texas; Shelvin' Rock/Old Mother Flanagan; Snake River Reel; Hard Traveling; John Stenson's #2; Roseville Fair; Front Porch Waltz.*

**New Frontier** (Blue rose 1001 CD) - All instrumentals w/Dan Levenson on banjo, fiddle and guitar and Kim Murley on hammered dulcimer and Yang Qin (Chinese hammered dulcimer). Tunes: *Kitchen Girl/Growling Old Man, Grumbling Old Woman; Weaving Girl; Lullaby; Pachinko; Liza Poor Gal/Traveling Down the Road; Dance of the Yao People; Red Haired Boy; Duke of Kent's Waltz; Thunder on a Dry Day; Horse Race; Flying Indian; Dragon Boat; Mackinac Bats; Rosy Cloud Follows the Moon; Song of the Frontier; Cherry Blossom Waltz.*

**Early Bird Special** (Buzzard 1004 CD) - Dan plays with The Boiled Buzzards Old Time Stringband. Tunes: *Smith's Reel; Beasties in the Sugar; Wooden Nickel; Brandywine/Three Forks of Reedy; The Engineers Don't Wave From the Train Anymore; Black Widow Romp; Young Guns and Miners; Boys Them Buzzards Are Flying; Lulu Loves Them Young; Bitter Creek; Lost Everything; Nixon's Farewell; Teabag Blues; Sadie at the Back Door/Waiting for Nancy; You Can't Get There From Here; Snake River Reel; Grey Haired Dancing Girl; Cliff's Waltz.* Mostly instrumental (vocals on 2 cuts) banjo, fiddle, guitar, and acoustic bass.

**Eat at Joe's** (Buzzard 1003 CD) - Dan plays with the Boiled Buzzards. Tunes: *Paddy on the Turnpike; John Brown's March/Waiting for the Federals; Snake River Reel; Hollow Poplar; Spotted Pony; Dinah/Wake Up Susan; Black Widow Romp; Katy Hill; Nixon's Farewell; Shady Grove; Spring in the Valley; Cuffy; The Year of Jubilo/Yellow Rose of Texas; Jimmy in the Swamp; Nixon's Farewell (w/double fiddles); Julianne Johnson; Tombigbee Waltz.* All instrumental music played on banjo, fiddle, guitar, and acoustic bass.

**Fine Dining** (Buzzard 1002 CD) - Dan plays with the Boiled Buzzards. Tunes: *Shuffle About; Little Dutch Girl; John Brown's Dream; Liza Jane; Goodbye Miss Liza; Booth Shot Lincoln; Briarpicker Brown; Monkey on a Dogcart; Fortune; Shenandoah Falls; Three Ponies; Jaybird; Forked Deer/Doctor Doctor; Leaving Home; Rock the Cradle Joe; Old Mother Flanagan; Santa Claus; Too Young to Marry; Roscoe; Stambaugh Waltz.* Mostly instrumental (vocals on 2 cuts) banjo, harmonica, guitar, and acoustic bass.

**Salt and Grease** (Buzzard 1001 CD) - is The Boiled Buzzards' first album. Tunes: *Julianne Johnson; 3 Thin Dimes; Durang's Hornpipe; Milwaukee Blues; Muddy Roads; Log Chain/Railroading Across the Rocky Mountains (Marmaduke's Hornpipe); Billy in the Lowground; Yellow Barber; Little Billy Wilson; Sandy Boys; Southtown; Rochester Schottische; Kansas City Reel; June Apple; Bull at the Wagon; Sally Ann Johnson; Nail That Catfish to a Tree; Icy Mountain; Benton's Dream; Sadie's Waltz.* Mostly instrumental (vocals on 2 cuts) banjo, harmonica, guitar, and acoustic bass.

For more information and to order Dan's products, please go to
*www.Clawdan.com*

# Old-Time Favorites for Clawhammer Banjo

is written by:
Dan N. Levenson

Feel free to contact him through the publisher or by e-mail at:
Clawdan@clawdan.com

You can also reach him on the web at:
http://www.Clawdan.com

**Dan Levenson** is a Southern Appalachian native who has grown up with the music of that region. Today he is considered a respected master teacher and performer of both the Clawhammer banjo & Appalachian style fiddle. *Banjo Newsletter*'s R.D. Lunceford describes Dan "as an interpreter, rather than a music re-creator". *Fiddler Magazine*'s Bob Buckingham described him as "an accomplished fiddler and ...one of the best clawhammer banjo players in the country." Ken Perlman has called him "The Johnny Appleseed of the banjo". He was also voted one of the top ten clawhammer players by Banjo Newsletter readers.

Dan has won awards on both instruments including first place at the 2005 *Ohio Clawhammer Banjo Championship* and Grand Champion at the 2010 *Ajo, AZ, fiddle contest*. He has over 10 recordings both with his band *The Boiled Buzzards* and as a solo artist.

Dan performs and teaches regularly throughout the country. He has taught at many of the traditional music schools and camps including the *Rolland Fiddle Camp, John C. Campbell Folk School, Mars Hill, Maryland Banjo Academy, The Ozark Folk Center* at Mountain View, AR, and *Banjo Camp North* among others. He also runs clawhammer banjo, fiddle and stringband workshops throughout the year.

Dan is an author for Mel Bay publications. His books include *Clawhammer Banjo From Scratch*; *Old Time Fiddle From Scratch*; *First Lessons Clawhammer Banjo*; *First Lessons Folk Banjo*; *Old Time Festival Tunes for Clawhammer Banjo*; *Old Time Festival Tunes for Fiddle & Mandolin*; *Gospel Tunes for Clawhammer Banjo*; *Kyle Creed Clawhammer Banjo Master*; *Wade Ward Clawhammer Banjo Master*; and *Buzzard Banjo Clawhammer Style*. He is also a writer and editor for *Banjo Newsletter's Old Time Way*.

To order Dan's books, recordings and for more information about Dan please go to
www.Clawdan.com